9/09

D1531317

Dolphins

By Valerie J. Weber

Reading Consultant: Susan Nations, M.Ed.,
author/literacy coach/consultant in literacy development

WEEKLY READER®
PUBLISHING

Please visit our web site at www.garethstevens.com.
For a free catalog describing our list of high-quality books,
call 1-800-542-2595 (USA) or 1-800-387-3178 (Canada).
Our fax: 1-877-542-2596

Library of Congress Cataloging-in-Publication Data

Weber, Valerie.
        Dolphins / by Valerie J. Weber.
                p. cm. — (Animals that live in the ocean)
        Includes bibliographical references and index.
        ISBN-10: 0-8368-9240-2   ISBN-13: 978-0-8368-9240-6 (lib. bdg.)
        ISBN-10: 0-8368-9339-5   ISBN 978-0-8368-9339-7 (softcover)
        1. Dolphins—Juvenile literature. I. Title.
QL737.C432W43   2008
599.53—dc22   2008009597

This edition first published in 2009 by
Weekly Reader® Books
An Imprint of Gareth Stevens Publishing
1 Reader's Digest Road
Pleasantville, NY 10570-7000 USA

Senior Managing Editor: Lisa M. Herrington
Senior Editor: Barbara Bakowski
Creative Director: Lisa Donovan
Designer: Alexandria Davis
Cover Designer: Amelia Favazza, *Studio Montage*
Photo Researcher: Diane Laska-Swanke

Photo Credits: Cover, pp. 1, 5, 11, 13, 15, 17, 19, 21 © SeaPics.com;
p. 7 Picture Quest; p. 9 © Jeff Rotman/naturepl.com

Printed in the United States of America

1 2 3 4 5 6 7 8 9 10 09 08

Table of Contents

Boldface words appear in the glossary.

A Mammal, Not a Fish

Like a fish, a dolphin lives in the water. A dolphin swims like a fish, but it is not a fish!

A dolphin is a **mammal**. It needs to breathe air, just as people do. A dolphin swims to the top of the water. Then the animal sucks in air through its **blowhole**.

blowhole

Like other mammals, dolphins give birth to live young. A baby dolphin is called a **calf**. A baby dolphin drinks milk from its mother's body.

calf

Time for Fun

Dolphins like to play. They race through the sea. They leap high out of the water.

Dolphins spin on their tails.
They also flip in circles.
Sometimes dolphins hit the
water hard with their bellies.

Speedy Swimmers

Dolphins chase fish, trying to catch them. A dolphin's speed helps it catch its **prey**. Prey are animals that are hunted and eaten.

15

Dolphins dig for small fish that hide under sand. A dolphin uses its strong **snout** to push at the ocean floor.

snout

Sharks often hunt for dolphins. With its sharp teeth, a shark sometimes takes a bite from a dolphin. The dolphin swims fast to escape.

shark bite

Making Some Noise

Dolphins often live in groups. They click and whistle to each other. Each dolphin in a group makes a different sound. It uses the same sound for its whole life.

Glossary

blowhole: an opening on top of a dolphin's head through which it breathes air

calf: a baby dolphin or other animal

mammal: a warm-blooded animal that has hair on its skin and that makes milk to feed its young

prey: animals that are eaten for food

snout: the front part of an animal's head, including its nose, mouth, and jaws

For More Information

Books

Diving Dolphin. Beginning to Read (series). Karen Wallace (DK Publishing, 2001)

Dolphins and Sharks. Magic Tree House Research Guide (series). Mary Pope Osborne and Natalie Pope Boyce (Random House Children's Books, 2003)

Web Sites

Defenders of Wildlife
www.defenders.org/wildlife_and_habitat/wildlife/ dolphin.php
Learn about different kinds of dolphins, how they grow, and what they eat.

Dolphins at Enchanted Learning
www.enchantedlearning.com/themes/dolphins.html
Find quizzes, activities, and information about dolphins.

Index

About the Author

A writer and editor for 25 years, Valerie Weber especially loves working in children's publishing. The variety of topics is endless, from weird animals to making movies. It is her privilege to try to engage children in their world through books.